From Money Stress to Money Strategy

Budget Like a Boss, Crush Debt & Build Wealth (Even if You're Starting from Zero!)

Nita Wolff

DEDICATION

Dedicated to my crushing debt from my 30's. Without it, I never would've changed my ways.

DISCLAIMER

The information provided in this book is based on my personal experience, research, and opinions. It is intended for general informational and educational purposes only and **does not constitute financial advice**.

I am not a licensed financial adviser, and this book does not take into account your specific financial situation or needs. You should always consult with a qualified financial professional before making any financial decisions.

While every effort has been made to ensure the accuracy of the information, I make no guarantees and assume no responsibility for any actions taken based on the content of this book.

If you are experiencing financial hardship, Financial Counsellors are available in every Australian state and territory, and they are 100% free.

Financial Counsellors can help people struggling with debt and money issues by assessing the situation, creating budgets, negotiating with creditors on your behalf (with your permission of course), and more. They don't give financial advice but instead empower you to manage bills, fines, mortgage stress, and credit card debt. All 100% free and confidential.

You can find a Financial Counsellor by doing a simple Google search for Financial Counsellors in your local area, call the National Debt Helpline on 1800 007 007 or use their website (www.ndh.org.au) to find local services.

CONTENTS

👋 Welcome!

You've just taken the first step toward financial clarity, confidence, and peace of mind.

This book is your no shame, no stress guide to budgeting, managing debt, and building wealth in small and manageable steps.

Whether you're starting over, stuck in a cycle of stress, or just want a clear plan, you're in the right place.

Let's make your **Money Stress** your **Money Strategy**.

Small steps everyday lead to big change.

✔ Your Progress Tracker

Tick each module as you complete it!

☐ Module 1: Your Money Mindset

☐ Module 2: The Snapshot

☐ Module 3: The 2 Hour Budget Reset

☐ Module 4: Debt Demolition

☐ Module 5: Smart Savings

☐ Module 6: Beginner Wealth

☐ Module 7: Your Strategy Game Plan

☐ Bonus 1: Quick Wins Toolkit

☐ Bonus 2: Emotional Spending SOS

☐ Bonus 3: Money Confidence Scripts

Module 1: Your Money Mindset

You don't need more willpower; you need a system.

📘 Why This Matters

Before we talk numbers, we need to talk about what's going on underneath. Most people don't struggle with money because they're lazy or irresponsible; they struggle because they've never been taught how to manage it in a way that works in real life.

That ends now.

This module is about gently resetting your relationship with money. We'll acknowledge what's been holding you back, without shame, and create a foundation of self-trust, calm, and clarity to build on.

Money is not just about math. It's about the emotions, habits, and stories we tell ourselves.

✨ What You'll Learn

- Why mindset matters more than motivation

- How your personal money story affects your current habits

- How to reframe guilt and reset your narrative

- How to write a powerful "Why" statement to guide you

🧠 What Is a Money Mindset?

Your **money mindset** is your *internal story about money*; how you think about it, feel about it, and respond to it. It's not just what you know about money. It's the beliefs, emotions, and patterns you carry that influence every financial decision you make.

Think of it this way. Two people can have the exact same income but very different outcomes, because of how they think and feel about money.

One person might see money as a tool for stability, while the other sees it as a source of stress or shame.

Your mindset shapes your choices: how you spend, save, avoid, or obsess over money.

🧬 Where Does Your Money Mindset Come From?

- **Family beliefs:** How your parents handled and talked about money (or didn't).

- **Childhood experiences:** Moments that made money feel safe, scarce, exciting, or shameful.

- **Cultural messages:** "Money is the root of all evil" or "Success equals wealth."

- **Personal wins and wounds:** Times you felt empowered... or totally overwhelmed.

You didn't choose these influences, but now that you're aware of them, *you get to reshape them.*

🔍 Why It Matters

You could have the best budget in the world, but if you secretly believe…

- "I'll never have enough"

- "I'm just not good with money"

- "Every time I try, I fail"

… then you'll subconsciously sabotage your progress, avoid taking action, or give up at the first setback.

This is why so many people struggle with money even if they *know* what to do. Mindset comes first.

💬 Examples of Limiting Money Beliefs

Do any of these sound familiar?

- "I'm just not a numbers person."

- "Money always disappears."

- "We weren't meant to be wealthy."

- "I'm no good at saving."

- "Money causes problems."

- "I'll never get ahead, so why bother?"

These aren't facts. They're beliefs, and beliefs can change.

✨ Your New Mindset Can Sound Like:

- ☑ "I'm learning how to take care of my money, even if it's messy right now."
- ☑ "I deserve stability and peace."
- ☑ "It's safe for me to look at my finances."
- ☑ "Money is a tool, not a test."
- ☑ "Small steps count."

📝 Journal Prompt

Take some time and answer honestly; there's no judgment here, just awareness.

1. My first memory of money is…

_____

_____

2. When I think about budgeting, I feel…

_____

_____

3. I used to believe money meant…

_____

_____

4. This is what's holding me back…

_____

_____

Now take a moment and answer this.

5. Instead, I want to believe…

_____

_____

_____

💡 Tip

Write freely. This is only for you.

Reframe: From Guilt to Growth

Reframing means learning to **look at a situation through a new lens**. It doesn't mean pretending things are perfect, it means choosing thoughts that are *more useful, less punishing,* and that help you move forward.

Most people have unhelpful thoughts around money that feel automatic. But here's the good news: **thoughts can be challenged and changed**, and when they change, so do our feelings, actions, and outcomes.

What Reframing Sounds Like

Here are some common internal scripts, and how to gently reframe them:

Guilty or Harsh Thought	Growth-Oriented Reframe
"I'm terrible with money."	"I was never taught how to manage money, but I'm learning now."
"I'll never get out of debt."	"Every payment moves me forward. This is a process, not a punishment."
"I keep messing up."	"I made a mistake, not an identity. I can learn from this."
"I'm just bad with numbers."	"I can build a system that works for *me*, even if I'm not a numbers person."
"I can't afford anything fun."	"I'm choosing to prioritise peace of mind right now, but fun is still part of my plan."

Reframing is about being honest AND kind. It helps you speak to yourself the way you would speak to a friend or loved one, with encouragement, not shame.

🔄 Try This: Reframe in Real Time

When you notice a thought that feels heavy, try this quick 3-step reset:

1. **Catch it:**
   Pause and notice the thought; don't judge it, just name it.
   → *"There's that 'I'm so bad with money' voice again."*

2. **Question it:**
   Ask: Is this thought true? Is it helpful? Where did it come from?
   → *"I'm not bad with money; I'm in a transition. I'm doing something about it."*

3. **Replace it:**
   Choose a gentler, more accurate thought that feels possible.
   → *"I'm building new habits. This takes time."*

✎ Journal Prompt

Think of a recent moment when you felt guilty, overwhelmed, or discouraged about money.

Write the thought you had below:

🧠 *Unhelpful thought:*

_____

_____

_____

_____

_____

_____

_____

_____

Now reframe it:

💡 *Supportive reframe:*

_____

_____

_____

_____

Repeat that reframe each time the old thought shows up.

You are literally rewiring your mindset, one sentence at a time.

✍️ Create Your "Why" Statement

Your **Why Statement** is the emotional anchor for your money reset.

It's not about goals like "save $500" or "pay off a credit card". Those are important, but they come later.

Your "why" is *why it matters to you personally* to reset your relationship with money.

It helps you keep going when it gets boring, hard, or slow.

💬 Why Your "Why" Works

- It makes the journey feel meaningful, not just practical.

- It gives you a reason to say "no" to things that don't serve you.

- It reminds you that this isn't about restriction, it's about freedom.

When you hit a hard day or a spending setback (because we all do), your "why" helps you get back on track, without guilt or spiraling.

💡 Real-Life "Why" Examples

Let these inspire your own Why. Your story is unique, but the feelings are shared:

💼 If you're burnt out:

"I'm resetting my money, so I don't have to stay in a job that drains me."

🧸 If you're a parent:

"I want to break the cycle of money stress for my kids."

🧠 If you've struggled with guilt or shame:

"I want to feel calm and capable when I open my bank app."

💳 If you're paying off debt:

"I want to be debt-free so I can finally breathe and make choices freely."

🏠 If you're rebuilding after hardship:

"I want to prove to myself that I can do this on my own."

Think about where you're at right now. What's frustrating, scary, or stressful about money? Imagine your life 6 months from now if you had a calm, clear, and working money system. What would feel better? Easier? More joyful?

Now, finish this sentence:

"I'm resetting my money because..."

✍️ Write Your Why

Use this space to write your Why Statement. Don't worry if it's messy; this is just for you. (And you get a chance to make it neater on the next page.)

📘 *I'm resetting my money because...*

_____

_____

_____

_____

🦺 Make It Visible

Once you write your "why," put it somewhere you'll see it regularly; your fridge, your planner, the lock screen on your phone, or inside your wallet. The more you see it, the more you'll **believe it, return to it, and act in alignment with it,** even on the hard days.

💡 Tip

When you're having a tough time, or feel like you're getting nowhere, repeat your Why like a mini mantra. **It will remind you of exactly why you're doing this!**

✍️ This is Your Why

Use this space to write your Why Statement.

Then rip out the page and put it somewhere you can see it all the time. You could even keep it in your wallet!

_____

_____

_____

_____

_____

_____

_____

_____

_____

_____

🌟

You've Got This!

You just did the most important work: you started.

You looked inward, got honest, and laid the groundwork for lasting change.

Everything that follows will build on this.

Keep going! You're doing better than you think. 💚

💡 Module 2: The Snapshot

Find out where you really stand, with zero shame or spreadsheets

📘 Why This Matters

Most people avoid the 3 B's; bills, bank statements, and budgeting, all because it feels overwhelming or shameful. But the truth is: **clarity is power**.

This step is not about judgment, it's about getting a clear, honest view of your finances so you can make grounded, confident decisions.

You don't need to fix everything today. You just need to *look*, and that's a powerful first step.

You can't change what you won't look at, so let's do it kindly.

✨ What You'll Learn

- How to take a simple snapshot of your financial life
- What to track (income, bills, debt, savings & assets) without being overwhelmed
- How to gather your numbers without shame

🔍 What Is a Money Snapshot?

A **Money Snapshot** is a clear, honest picture of your current financial situation, taken at a single point in time, just like that selfie in your camera roll.

Think of it like pressing *pause* on your money and taking a screenshot of where things stand today.

It doesn't have to be perfect. It doesn't have to be pretty. It just has to be *real*.

📷 It's a Photo, not a Report Card

A snapshot is not a judgment. It's not your worth. And it's not a permanent label.

It's a simple way of saying *"Here's where I am right now. Let's build from here."*

It's the difference between guessing and *knowing*. Once you know what's really going on, you can start to:

- Make more confident decisions

- Set realistic goals

- Spot easy wins or budget "leaks"

- Feel more in control (even if things aren't perfect yet)

🧱 What Goes into Your Snapshot?

Your snapshot has four basic building blocks:

💰 **Income** — what's coming in regularly

💵 **Expenses** — what's going out regularly

📉 **Debts** — what you owe

📈 **Savings & Assets** — what you own

You can include as much or as little detail as you like, but the point is clarity, not overload.

🧠 Why This Step is So Powerful

Most people avoid this step because they're scared of what they'll see. But here's what they don't realise:

- **Clarity calms your nervous system**
  Your brain can stop running in circles once it sees real numbers.

- **Knowing your numbers gives you choices**
  You can't plan with fog. You can plan with facts.

- **It's the starting point for everything**
  Your budget, your goals, your savings; they all build from this.

Even if your snapshot shows a mess, at least now you know. That's what gives you power and progress.

💬 Real Talk: "But My Numbers Are a Mess"

So? That's totally normal. Most people's numbers *are* a mess!

The goal right now isn't to have perfect numbers, it's to be brave enough to *look*.

Here's what to do if that fear creeps in:

- Take on one section at a time. This isn't a race or a test; this is just for you.

- Estimate if needed. You don't need to know everything down to the exact cent, just a round figure will work.

- Remind yourself: **You are allowed to learn as you go.**

✨ What You'll Feel After Taking Your Snapshot

- ☑ **Relief** thanks to no more guesswork

- ☑ **Empowerment** now that you're facing your money like a boss!

- ☑ **Motivation** because now you know what needs fixing (and what's already working)

- ☑ **A strong foundation** for every financial decision to come

🦄 Let's Bust a Myth

Do you find yourself saying *"I'll feel better once I fix everything"*?

Actually? No, sorry, that's not true.

You'll feel better once you stop hiding from your money!

Even if the numbers aren't great (and for many people, they aren't), the relief of *knowing* outweighs the fear of guessing. Once you know where you're at, you can begin to make plans.

So, let's get to it!

🗃️ Step 1: Gather Your Info

Use this checklist to collect what you need:

- ☐ Pay slips or Centrelink income
- ☐ Recent bills (utilities, phone, rent, etc.)
- ☐ Debt statements (credit cards, loans, buy now/pay later)
- ☐ Savings or bank account balances
- ☐ Subscriptions (Spotify, Netflix, cloud storage, etc.)
- ☐ Any cash flow extras (child support, side hustles, etc.)
- ☐ Any known expense extras (upcoming car maintenance, etc.)

No need to be perfect; estimates are okay for now. The goal is visibility, not perfection.

📋 Step 2: Fill in Your Snapshot

In the following pages (or a notebook), set up four simple sections:

💰 **Income** (per week, fortnight or month)
- ○ Job income
- ○ Centrelink or other payments
- ○ Side hustles / extra sources

💵 **Expenses**
- ○ Rent/mortgage
- ○ Bills, subscriptions
- ○ Fuel, groceries, childcare, medical, etc.

📉 **Debts**
- ○ Credit cards
- ○ Personal loans
- ○ Buy Now, Pay Later
- ○ Any payment plans

📈 **Savings & Assets**
- ○ Emergency fund
- ○ Goal fund (e.g. Holiday)
- ○ Sinking fund
- ○ Investment accounts
- ○ Superannuation (optional)

💡 Tip

Not sure where to put something? Just guess. This isn't a test.

Snapshot Worksheet

Date of Snapshot: _____

This worksheet is your moment-in-time overview of your current money situation. No shame. Just facts.

💰 1. Income

What's coming in (per week, fortnight or month — your choice)

Source	Amount ($)	Frequency
Main job / wages		
Centrelink / benefits		
Side hustle		
Child support / other		

Total Income

🔼 2. Expenses

Regular bills, essentials, and non-negotiables

Expense Type	Amount ($)	Frequency
Rent / Mortgage		
Electricity		
Gas		
Phone & Internet		
Transport / Fuel		
Groceries		
Insurance		
Medical / Medication		
Kids / Pets / School		
Other		

Total Expenses

💡 Tip

Start with what you know. Use bank statements, your calendar, or app screenshots.

🔻 3. Debt Overview

What you owe — no judgment, just clarity

Lender / Account	Balance Owing ($)	Min. Repayments ($)	Interest Rate (%)
Credit Card			
Personal Loan			
Afterpay / ZipPay			
Centrelink			
Car Loan			
Other			

Total Debt

✨ **Reminder:** I know this section can feel heavy. Looking at your debts is a daunting task.

But you've done something brave by facing it.

It's going to be okay. **Clarity is power**, and you've just taken the first step to *reclaiming* your power.

📈 4. Savings & Assets

What you own, even if it's small — it all counts

Account / Type	Balance ($)	Notes
Emergency Fund		
General Savings		
Goal Fund		e.g. Car, Holiday
Investments (ETFs, shares)		
Superannuation		
Cash on hand		
Other		

Total Savings

🔍 Step 3: Reflect

Look over your snapshot.

Don't panic. Don't criticise. Just observe.

🧘 Ask yourself:

- "What surprised me?"

- "What's working okay already?"

- "Where is my money actually going?"

- "What do I want to change?"

🧠 Reframing Reminder

If shame creeps in, reframe your thoughts and come back to this:

"I'm not behind, I'm getting clear. This is progress."

✅ Action Step

You've completed your Money Snapshot, had some time to really look at all four building blocks, and reflect on those numbers.

Take a breath. What stands out?

🖋 Something I didn't expect:

_____

🖋 Something I'm proud of:

_____

🖋 One thing I'd like to change:

_____

Now let's put it all together and write a one-line summary:

📘 My biggest insight from this snapshot is...

_____
_____
_____
_____

⭐

You've Got This!

You did the bravest part; you looked!

Now instead of spinning in guilt or guessing, you have clarity. That's your launchpad for everything that comes next.

A snapshot gives you the truth, the truth gives you choices, and choices give you freedom.

💰 Module 3: The 2-Hour Budget Reset

A realistic budget you'll actually stick to, even if your income is all over the place

👋 Welcome to Your Reset

This is your turning point.

You've explored your mindset (module 1), faced your real numbers (module 2), and now it's time to build a strategy, *your strategy*.

This isn't about becoming a budgeting robot. It's about using your money with **clarity and purpose**, so you can finally breathe and start moving forward.

This method works whether you:

- Get paid weekly, fortnightly, or monthly

- Have a regular or irregular income

- Are brand new to budgeting

- Have tried before and "failed" (you haven't)

This is simple, intentional, and completely yours.

⏰ Why 2 Hours?

Because that's all you need to build a starting point. Not a perfect plan. Not a forever budget. Just a clear strategy you can use *right now*.

You don't have to track every cent or use a fancy app. You just need to take back control.

This reset is a repeatable process you can come back to any time things feel messy again.

✨ What You'll Learn

- How to choose a budget style that suits you

- What to do if your income changes each period

- How to plan for irregular expenses

- Tips for staying on track without getting stuck

⚙️ Choose a Budgeting Style That Suits You

There's no "best" budget. There's only the best budget that *works* for you. Pick a style that fits your brain, your energy, and your current lifestyle.

📋 Zero-Based Budgeting

Best for: People who like structure, detail, and knowing where every dollar goes.

With this method, you assign *every dollar a job*. You start with your income, subtract expenses, savings, and debt payments, and aim to bring the balance to zero. That doesn't mean spending everything, it means *every dollar is accounted for*.

> **Example:** If you bring in $2,000 this month, you might assign $1,200 to bills, $300 to groceries, $200 to savings, $200 to debt, and $100 to fun.

Why it works: You'll never wonder "where did my money go?" again. Every dollar has a job, and it's working!

Watch out for: It can feel intense at first, but you can keep it simple.

And don't sweat it if you end up with a "negative" balance at first. You just need to tweak your numbers a little in the areas that can be flexible, such as fun money or your takeaway fund.

⚖️ 50-30-20 Rule

Best for: People who want a straightforward plan without thinking too hard.

This method splits your after-tax income into three chunks:

- 50% Needs: rent, food, utilities, transport, debt

- 30% Wants: dining out, entertainment, shopping

- 20% Goals: savings, extra debt payments, investing

  💬 **Example:** If you earn $2,000/month, then $1,000 covers needs, $600 goes to wants, and $400 goes to savings or extra debt payments.

Why it works: Easy to remember, great for beginners, and very flexible.

Watch out for: You may need to adjust the ratios if your cost of living is high or your income is tight. Some circumstances will mean you need 60% in needs, so feel free to adjust the percentages as you need for your specific situation.

Some people do 70-20-10, or 80-20-0. It's all based on *your needs*, so make it your own.

💸 Cash Envelope System

Best for: People who overspend on cards or need tangible limits.

This one is very basic. All you do is take out cash and divide it into envelopes or ziplock bags labelled for each category, e.g. groceries, petrol, takeaway, etc. When the envelope is empty, that's it until next payday. This method can also work digitally by using prepaid gift cards for each category.

> ⋯ **Example:** $150 for groceries goes into a "Groceries" envelope. You shop using that amount (and only that amount) for the pay period.

Why it works: Physically seeing your money go down helps curb overspending.

Watch out for: Cash systems can be hard with online shopping or shared budgets, so sometimes prepaid gift cards can be a better solution. But this can also be tricky.

In that case, you need to watch out for extra fees and charges that shops may impose for using eftpos, both in store and online. Plus, the cost of the gift cards themselves. Let's not waste our hard-earned money just to buy a *piece of plastic*.

🧮 Bucket or Account-Based Budgeting

Best for: People who like visual organisation or use separate bank accounts.

You set up multiple bank accounts, each one for a different purpose. For example:

- Bills account

- Everyday spending account

- Emergency savings account

- Goal funds account (e.g. new car, holidays)

You then split your income into those accounts and spend accordingly. It's very similar to the Cash Envelope System, but instead relies on your bank accounts rather than physical cash.

> 💬 **Example:** You set up auto-transfers each payday: $900 to your bills account, $300 to spending, $100 to savings.

Why it works: Makes it easy to "set and forget" your budget. You can even integrate it with other methods, like the 50-30-20 Rule.

Watch out for: Too many accounts can feel confusing, plus you could end up paying fees over multiple banks. If you want to try this method, make sure you do your research first. There are plenty of fee-free bank accounts available through many different banks and credit unions.

You may need to read some fine print, but it's worth it to ensure you're not losing money for the "privilege" of having a bank account or two.

🍱 Flexible Hybrid Method

Best for: Most real-life humans, like you!

This is a mix-and-match approach where you use pieces of different systems to suit your life. For example:

- Automate bills and savings (like buckets)

- Track variable spending manually (like envelopes)

- Use 50-30-20 for monthly planning

- Check in weekly to tweak as needed

  … **Example:** You automate your rent, groceries and debt payments, and manually manage fun spending using a spending tracker.

Why it works: It adapts as your life changes, which is ideal if you're neurodiverse, managing variable income, or just hate rigidity.

Watch out for: You still need some structure; make sure this method is working, not just flexible.

❓ Not Sure Where to Start?

Try this:

- If you've never budgeted before, start with **50-30-20** to get a feel for your flow.

- If money slips through your fingers, try **cash envelopes** for one or two categories.

- If you want total clarity, go for a **zero-based budget** with automation.

- If you're overwhelmed by structure, build a **hybrid** that gives you permission to keep it simple.

🎯 *Your budget is allowed to be messy, change over time, and get easier with practice.*

🧮 Use Your Snapshot Numbers to Build a Working Strategy

From module 2, you now know your income, expenses, debts and savings. Now we're turning that into a real-life budget, one that helps you:

- Cover your essentials

- Stay on top of bills

- Put money toward goals

- Still have a life (without guilt)

🛠️ Build Your Beginner Budget

Use the **Beginner Budget Template** on the next page to:

- Set up your income and expense totals

- Identify categories where you could cut back slightly

- Plan for at least one goal fund (like gifts, car rego, or vet bills)

Beginner Budget Template

Expense	Amount ($)

Total $

Income	
Main Job / Wages	$
Centrelink	$
Side Hustle	$
Other	$

Total Income	$
Total Expenses	$
Leftover	$

⚙️ Choose Your Tools

Once you've built your budget, you can choose how to *run* your budget.

Some ideas:

- **Automate** bills & savings with scheduled transfers

- Use a **weekly planner** or **whiteboard** to track payments and goals

- **Stick to cash** if overspending is a trigger (this is a psychological trick; when you see the cash dwindling, you're less likely to spend)

- Set up **separate accounts** for category spending (e.g. bills account, savings account, daily spending account)

✨ **Reminder:** Tools don't fix money problems, clarity and consistency do.

💼 But my Income Changes Weekly / Fortnightly / Monthly

Budgeting on a rollercoaster income doesn't have to feel chaotic. If your income fluctuates, from shift work, gig work, commissions, or freelancing, you're not alone. The key is to **build your budget around your lowest consistent income**, not your best month.

For example, if your monthly income ranges from $2,000 to $3,000, set your budget based on $2,000. That ensures you always cover the essentials, even in slow months. When you earn more, you can allocate the extra to savings, extra debt payments, or upcoming expenses.

It also helps to separate your income from your spending. One simple trick: use a holding account where all your income lands, then "pay yourself" a steady amount for your spending, like a wage.

✅ Action Step

Look back at your last 3–6 months of income.

🖊 What's your **lowest reliable weekly / fortnightly / monthly income?**

$ _____

Use this number to build your next budget.

🔄 Set a Regular Check-In Schedule

Budgeting isn't one and done. But it doesn't have to be exhausting either. If you set yourself a regular check-in time, you will continue to *know* where your money is going, rather than having to guess if you have enough to buy that extra latte or lunch out with your friends.

Yes, even with budgeting you're still allowed to treat yourself! You earned this money; you can use it however you want!

As my lovely wife likes to say, **you're an adult with adult money**. Have cake for dinner if you want!

Choose how often you'll check in:

Frequency	Works For
Weekly	If your pay or spending changes often
Fortnightly	Great for most Aussie pay cycles
Monthly	Best if you're stable and prefer less admin

🖊 I'll check in with my budget every:

☐ **Week**   ☐ **Fortnight**   ☐ **Month**

Set a calendar reminder or pair it with payday!

📅 How to Plan for Irregular Expenses

The "surprises" you actually knew were coming.

Ever feel like your budget keeps getting sideswiped by car rego, back-to-school costs, or Christmas? These are **irregular expenses**; not monthly, but predictable. Instead of getting caught out, you can set up **sinking funds**: small amounts you regularly set aside for these known costs.

Essentially, think of a sinking fund as a temporary savings account. You know the end goal is to have enough money to pay for that big expense, and if you put small amounts aside regularly, you can get there in however long you have until that expense is due.

The real difference between a sinking fund and a true savings account is that instead of a goal amount, you're working towards a due date. Because we all know bills should be paid when they're due.

> 💬 **Example:** Your car rego and CTP insurance is $800 this year (yes, I know, it's usually more than that but hear me out) and it's due in March next year.
>
> We're currently in May and you get paid fortnightly. So, you have approximately 20 pay periods to save up the payment.
>
> $$\$800 \div 20 \text{ pay periods} = \$40$$
>
> Savings $40 per fortnight means the **money's ready when you need it**.

You can create sinking funds for holidays, regular vet bills, Christmas, sports fees, or anything you know is coming. These aren't true savings accounts; they're bill management techniques and **they will** keep you on track.

✅ Action Step

Write down 5 – 10 irregular expenses you know are coming up over the next year, how much they'll cost, and when they're due.

✏️ E.g. *Car rego | $800 | March*

✏️ _____

✏️ _____

✏️ _____

✏️ _____

✏️ _____

✏️ _____

✏️ _____

✏️ _____

✏️ _____

Divide each expense by the number of pay cycles you have before it's due, and that's your sinking fund target per pay!

Total Sinking Fund ($) ÷ number of pay cycles = Target per Pay ($)

🧭 Tips for Staying on Track Without Getting Stuck

Progress is built on grace, not perfection.

Budgeting isn't about doing it perfectly; it's about staying connected. If you overspend or fall off track, don't scrap the whole plan. Just reset and keep going. Would you scrap your whole car if you got a flat tyre?

One helpful tool is adding a "**miscellaneous**" buffer (about 5 - 10% of your budget) to catch those little things that don't fit neatly into categories.

> 💬 **Example:** You've budgeted for groceries, bills, and rent, but then your child brings home a permission slip for a $25 school excursion you didn't see coming. It's not an emergency, it's not a big-ticket item, but it's enough to throw off your budget if you haven't allowed for it.

That's exactly what your **miscellaneous buffer** is for, those small and irregular expenses that are *predictable in theory*, but unpredictable in timing.

Other common examples include:

- A last-minute birthday gift
- Needing to grab a taxi, Uber or pay parking fees
- Replacing a broken phone charger

A buffer of just **$10 - $30 per pay cycle** can absorb these bumps without derailing your whole plan. Plus, it accumulates if you don't need to use it!

It's also powerful to track your progress visually. Whether you colour in a tracker or tally no-spend days, small reminders help you stay engaged. Most importantly, avoid all-or-nothing thinking.

Every step counts, even the wobbly ones.

⭐

You've Got This!

Budgeting isn't about deprivation. It's about direction.

This reset gives you clarity, structure, and a fresh start, whether it's your first budget or your fifteenth.

There's no shame in adjusting, restarting, or learning as you go. You're doing it!

Module 4: Debt Demolition

You're not bad with money, you've just been stuck in a system built for you to fail. Let's break out of that system!

📘 Why This Matters

Debt can feel heavy. Draining. Embarrassing. Overwhelming. But here's what most budgeting books don't tell you:

You did what you were *programmed* to do.

Every day we're bombarded with offers of interest free financing, no repayments for 24 months, limited time offers; all perfectly crafted to brainwash you into *needing* that item, *needing* that credit.

Now, you're doing something different.

This module is about taking your power back, with no shame. Whether you've got $500 or $500,000 in debt, the tools inside this module will help you make a plan, take action, and start feeling hope again.

Debt is often a survival strategy, not a failure.

✨ What You'll Learn

- The difference between the **Snowball**, **Avalanche**, and **Fireball** methods
- Why momentum matters more than math
- How to track and celebrate every payment
- How to negotiate lower rates or fees

🔄 Mindset Shift: From Shame to Strategy

Let's name a few truths:

- You are not your credit score.

- You are not your past financial decisions.

- You *are* allowed to start again (as many times as needed actually).

Debt is a **math problem with emotional roots**. And this module helps with both.

📊 Get Clear on What You Owe

You've already gathered your debts in Module 2. Let's bring them here for clarity. Copy your list into the **Debt Snapshot Worksheet** added at the end of this module or use this space below:

Account	Balance ($)	Interest Rate (%)	Min Payment ($)	Due Date

🎯 Pick a Paydown Strategy That Fits You

There's no one right way to tackle debt. The best method is the one you'll stick with.

Let's look at your options.

❄️ Snowball Method – Build Momentum

How it works: Paying the smallest to largest debts builds momentum fast.

1. List all your debts from smallest to largest **by balance**, ignoring the interest rates.

2. Pay the minimums on all debts.

3. Throw any extra money at the **smallest** debt first.

4. Once it's paid off, roll that payment onto the next smallest (like a snowball gaining size and speed).

Why it works: The snowball method is all about **psychological wins**. Paying off a debt (even a small one) gives you a dopamine boost, builds confidence, and creates visible progress early on.

> **Example:** You have the following debts;

- $300 store card at 17% interest
- $1200 credit card at 19.99% interest
- $3000 personal loan 23% interest

You'd attack the $300 debt first (even if the other cards/loans have higher interest rates) to get that **quick win**.

Best for: People who need motivation, fast wins, or who feel overwhelmed and need to **build momentum** and belief.

🏔 Avalanche Method – Save on Interest

How it works: Paying the highest interest to lowest will save the most interest over time.

1. List all your debts by **interest rate**, highest to lowest.

2. Pay the minimums on all debts.

3. Apply extra money to the **debt with the highest interest rate** first.

4. When that's gone, tackle the next highest interest rate debt, and so on.

Why it works: Mathematically, the avalanche method saves you the most money in the long run because you eliminate high-interest costs first.

Example: You have the following debts;

- $1500 credit card at 19.99% interest
- $2000 store loan at 12% interest
- $800 loan from your parents at 0% interest

You'd start with the $1500 card, because interest is eating up your money there. Then, once that debt was eliminated, you would work on the $2000 store loan as it's the next highest interest rate.

The $800 loan from your parents would be the very last to be paid, as it isn't incurring any interest and therefore not costing you anything extra the longer it takes to pay off.

Best for: Those who are motivated by **logic and long-term savings**, and who can stick to a plan even if it takes a while to see results.

☀️ Firestorm Method – Emotional Target

How it works: Paying a high stress debt can free up cash fast while also decreasing your emotional stress levels.

1. Identify any debts with **high minimum repayments** or that are causing **financial and emotional stress**.

2. Pay the minimums on all debts.

3. Prioritise clearing **those debts first** to **free up income quickly**.

4. Then switch to Snowball or Avalanche with the extra cash you've unlocked.

Why it works: This method is about **relieving pressure now**, especially if one debt is **dominating your paycheck**. It gives you space to breathe and reduces the chance of missing payments.

> **Example:** You have the following debts;

- $2000 credit card at 19.99% paying $60/month
- $4000 car loan at 11.5% paying $350/month
- $1000 payday loan at 49.5% paying $100/week (yes, that's an accurate interest rate on a payday loan)

You might focus on clearing the $1000 payday loan first not just because of the excessive interest, but because that $100 every week is **hurting your budget** and it's keeping you up at night.

Best for: People with **limited cash flow**, juggling multiple repayments, or feeling the **strain of high minimums**.

Journal Prompt

Which strategy feels like the best fit for my debts, and why?

_____

_____

_____

_____

_____

_____

📋 Make Your Plan

Once you've chosen your method, these are the steps to follow:

✅ Step 1:

<u>This is the most important step.</u> No matter what, keep paying the minimum on all your debts. If you don't, you may get defaults or have debt collectors come knocking, and no one has time for that!

✅ Step 2:

Choose your target debt based on which method you have chosen. E.g. **Snowball** = Smallest Balance, **Avalanche** = Highest Interest Rate, **Firestorm** = Most Stressful.

✅ Step 3:

Throw every spare dollar you can at it, while still paying your regular minimum repayments.

That's it. That's the entire strategy.

Once your targeted debt is paid off, you just restart from step 1 for the next debt. Easy as!

💡 Tip

Use your budget to find the spare dollars for paying your debts. This could be from leftover spending money, subscriptions you paused or cancelled, side hustle income, or tax returns. Even $20 extra per pay can make a difference.

🚗 Why Momentum Matters More Than Math

When you're paying off debt, the best plan isn't always the one that saves the most interest; it's the one you'll stick with.

Progress builds motivation, and motivation fuels *consistency*. That's why knocking over a small $200 debt often works better than attacking a big, high-interest one first.

Every quick win boosts your confidence, proving to your brain that you *can* do this. In the real world, emotion drives action more than logic, and for many people, starting with what feels doable is the key to not giving up.

So don't worry if your method isn't the most "mathematically optimal." If it keeps you moving, **it's working**.

Seeing your debt go down can be incredibly motivating, so try:

- A printable debt tracker to colour in

- A progress bar on your fridge

- A savings/debt jar you add coins to

- Banking app nicknames like "**BYE CREDIT CARD**"

- A monthly milestone log

🎉 Celebrate the Wins

Every time you:

- Pay off a balance

- Lower your interest

- Avoid a late fee

- Make your first extra payment

- Reduce stress around your debt

...you are winning!

Even if it's slow. Even if you have setbacks.

Debt freedom isn't a destination. It's a direction.

Debt Snapshot Worksheet

Instructions: Use this worksheet to capture every debt you currently owe (make copies if you need more space). Remember, this is about gaining clarity, not judgment. Once it's all in front of you, you can make a plan to move forward.

Debt 1:			
Debt Type	Lender / Provider	Balance Owing	Due Date / Term
		$	
Min Payment	Interest rate	Notes	Strategy
$	%		

Debt 2:			
Debt Type	Lender / Provider	Balance Owing	Due Date / Term
		$	
Min Payment	Interest rate	Notes	Strategy
$	%		

Debt 3:			
Debt Type	Lender / Provider	Balance Owing	Due Date / Term
		$	
Min Payment	Interest rate	Notes	Strategy
$	%		

🌟

You've Got This!

You are not behind.
You are not broken.
You are not failing.

You are **actively dismantling a system that no longer serves you**; one payment, one choice, one step at a time.

🎓 Module 5: Smart Savings

Your first emergency fund: why it's non-negotiable!

📘 Why This Matters

Savings is about *safety*, not perfection. Even a small emergency fund changes everything. It gives you breathing room, keeps you from reaching for a credit card every time life throws a curveball, and helps you break the cycle of living paycheck to paycheck.

This isn't about saving thousands right away; it's about proving to yourself that you *can* save. Once you do that, it becomes easier to keep going.

Your first $1,000 saved is your financial seatbelt. It doesn't prevent the crash; it protects you when it happens.

✨ What You'll Learn

- Why $1000 is the first milestone

- Simple ways to build savings, even on a tight income

- How to automate your savings so you don't have to think about it

- Fun savings challenges that actually work!

🎯 Let's Talk Goals

Everyone knows goal setting can be a real pain in the proverbial, but without goals how do we know which direction to head? Sure, we could just pick a number and go for it, but without a *why* (just like in module 1), we're not going to stick to it.

There's no perfect number when it comes to savings goals, but here's a great place to start:

Goal	Why It Helps
$500	Handles minor unexpected costs (bills, repairs, school)
$1,000	Your true starter emergency fund which protects you from falling into debt
1 Month of Expenses	More security between jobs, life changes, or slow income

💵 Why $1000 is the First Milestone

Your starter emergency fund is more powerful than you think.

If you're just beginning, saving **$1,000** might feel like climbing a mountain, but it's one of the most impactful steps you can take. This small cushion creates a **critical buffer between you and financial chaos**. It's not about covering every possible emergency. It's about **breaking the cycle of debt** when life throws you a curveball.

Without a savings buffer, even a relatively small expense (like a flat tire, a vet bill, or a broken fridge) can push you back into credit card debt or payday loans. But with $1,000 ready to go, you've got breathing room. It buys you time. It gives you choices. And most importantly, it **proves to yourself that you can save**.

🚨 Real-Life Example:

"Emma" is living paycheck to paycheck. One day, she has a minor car accident. No one is hurt, but it does just enough damage that she needs to make an insurance claim for repairs. The insurance company is happy to process her claim, and she must pay her insurance excess of $750 before repairs can begin at the mechanic.

Without savings, she would've had to use a credit card or take a small payday loan, adding more debt to an already tight budget. But because she had her starter $1,000 emergency fund, she paid the $750 bill stress-free. She was still safe, still stable and (most importantly) *still in control*.

✅ Action Step

Pick one savings goal to focus on this month. It doesn't have to be to have a $1000 emergency fund or anything huge. The point is to begin; **momentum** comes from **clarity.**

🖊 My goal is...

_____

_____

_____

_____

Now, let's make it happen!

⚙️ Choose Your Saving Method

There's no perfect savings method, just the one that fits your life right now. Here are three beginner-friendly approaches to choose from. Pick one, or combine them to create your custom method:

🪙 1. Daily Micro-Saves

This method involves saving a small amount **every day**, typically between $1 and $5. It's perfect if you're working with a tight income or want to build the habit of saving without feeling it. You can use a money jar for cash, transfer to a high-interest savings account, or an app that lets you set daily goals.

Why it works: Small daily habits add up fast and help you form a saving identity; you become someone who *always* saves, even a little.

> 💬 **Example:** Save $3/day × 30 days = $90/month

Tips to make it easier:

- Set a daily phone reminder
- Link it to a habit you already have (e.g. save right after brushing your teeth)
- Use a visual tracker or sticker chart to see your streak

📌 Try This:

Set a 10-day goal: "I'll save $3 a day for 10 days = $30."

✏️ Daily amount: $_____ | Start date: _____

Tiny amounts. Big results.

🔄 2. Round-Ups

Round-up saving means **automatically rounding up each purchase** to the nearest dollar and moving the "spare change" into savings. You remember that spot in your parents' car that was always full of coins? It's the same thing. They put their spare change from all kinds of purchases into that one spot, just like you can do with your spare change into a savings or investing account. Some banks and apps even offer this as a built-in feature, so *no effort required!*

Why it works: It's invisible, automatic, and painless. You don't have to *do* anything; it just happens every time you spend.

> 💬 **Example:** You buy lunch for $8.40 → 60c goes to savings
> Do this 5–10 times a week = approx. $5–$10 saved weekly

Where to find it: Check your bank's app or use third-party savings or investing apps that support round-up features.

📌 Try This:

Turn on round-ups in your banking/investing/savings app. Track how much builds up in 2 weeks. You'll be surprised how much "spare change" can grow.

✏️ App used: _____ | First transfer: $_____

And if you use cash, do what your parents did; put your "spare change" in a spot like a jar on the fridge, a bowl near the front door, or **yes even your car**; and watch it overflow.

Save your spare change, effortlessly.

🔀 3. Auto-Transfer

Automated transfers are a savings game-changer. Set up a **recurring payment** from your everyday account to your savings account (ideally one that's separate and not easy to dip into).

> 💬 **Example:** $25 every week → $100/month → $1,200/year!

Why it works: It removes emotion and decision fatigue. You're not waiting until money is "left over". You're making savings a **priority**, just like those important bills like rent or groceries. Make *paying yourself* a bill.

Tips for success:

- Automate on payday or the next day
- Use an account with withdrawal restrictions (like losing bonus interest) to avoid temptation
- Start small with your regular deposits and increase the amount later once you're in a routine

📌 Try This:

Log into your online banking and set up a $/week transfer. It doesn't have to be hundreds. Start small, say $5, and increase it once you're in a routine.

🖊 Weekly amount: $_____ | Start date: _____

Treat savings like a bill and pay yourself first.

📑 Bonus Method: Combo Plan

Can't pick just one? Use a **hybrid approach**. Maybe you automate $20 per week, round-up purchases, and do micro-saves of $3 per weekday. This adds variety and keeps it fun.

> 💬 **Example:** Auto-Transfers → $20 every week → $80/month → $960/year
>
> Plus: Round-ups → $7 every week → $28/month → $336/year
>
> Plus: Daily Micro-Saves → $15 every week → $60/month → $720/year
>
> So, $960 + $336 + $720 = **$2016 SAVED!**

Why it works: It makes saving fun!

📌 **Try This:**

✏️ Which methods could you combine?

- ☐ Micro-saves
- ☐ Round-ups
- ☐ Auto-transfer

✏️ My combo: _____

🎲 Saving Challenges That Actually Work

Saving doesn't have to feel boring or hard. Make it a game and you'll stick with it longer.

Saving money can feel like a chore and be boring, but when you turn it into a challenge, it becomes something to win at. And we all love to win.

Saving challenges use **short-term goals, small wins, and visual progress** to keep you motivated. They're ideal when you're just getting started or trying to break through a plateau.

Challenges also help rewire your brain: they shift the focus from sacrifice to strategy. It becomes less about what you're "giving up" and more about what you're building.

🏁 Choose a Challenge That Fits You

Here are four tried-and-true challenges to get you started:

🪜 1. Step-Up Challenge

Save a little more each week for 10 weeks.

Week	Save	Total
1	$5	$5
2	$10	$15
3	$15	$30
4	$20	$50
...	...	...
10	$50	$275

Best for: Building momentum over time.

💡 Tip

Adjust the amounts if the above example is too high. You can start at $2 and increase by $2 weekly instead. Really, you can start at any amount and increase by any amount you like, just keep it consistent and *it will work*!

🚫 2. No-Spend Challenge

Pick a day (or week, or month) where you spend *nothing* outside of essentials. And at the end of the day (or week, or month), put your leftover money into your savings.

You'll be surprised how much you save just by **pausing spending habits**. It also builds awareness of emotional or impulse purchases.

> ⋯ **Example:** No spending on weekdays for 2 weeks = $ saved plus your mindset shifted.

Best for: Curbing overspending and resetting habits.

💡 Tip

Give yourself a reward *that isn't spending* like a movie night at home, or a savings goal thermometer to colour in.

🪙 3. $5 or Gold Coin Challenge

Every time you receive a $5 note or a $2 coin, put it into a savings jar or envelope. It's old school, and **it works**. This is an easy passive challenge that adds up quickly over time.

Best for: Cash users or those who want a tactile method. It's also a great method for kids when you're teaching them to save money.

💡 Tip

Use a jar or envelope that's visible; seeing it fill up keeps you engaged

🎨 4. Thematic Challenges

Savings, but with a twist like:

- **Alphabet Challenge:** Save something starting with A - Z (e.g. A = $1, B = $2... Z = $26 = $351 total), then move onto saving the amount of a word (e.g. "Cash" would be C = $3, A = $1, S = $19, H = $8 = $31 total)

- **52-Week Challenge:** Save $1 in Week 1, $2 in Week 2... up to $52 in Week 52 = $1,378/year

- **Pantry Challenge:** Go into your pantry and fridge, and only use what you already have for a few days of meals. Then bank the grocery savings.

These bring novelty and fun to the process!

✅ Action Step

📋 Plan Your First Challenge. Which challenge will you try first?

☐ Step-Up Challenge
☐ No-Spend Challenge
☐ $5 Note or $2 Coin Challenge
☐ Alphabet Challenge
☐ Other: _____

Start Date: _____

Goal Amount: $_____

Reward When Completed: _____

🏁 Try This: The 10-Day Mini Savings Challenge

This quick-start challenge is designed to help you find and save **$100+ in 10 days** without overwhelming yourself.

Day	Task	Amount
1	Skip one takeout or coffee	$10
2	Sell one item online	$20
3	No-spend day	$10
4	Transfer spare account balance	$5
5	Round up every purchase today	$5
6	Cancel or pause one unused subscription	$15
7	Use a voucher or discount and bank the savings	$5
8	Cook a "pantry meal" from what you already have	$10
9	Use cashback or rewards to add to savings	$10
10	Transfer whatever you can manage today	$10+
	Total Saved	**$100+**

✅ *Set this up as a checklist or copy the idea into your Notes app and tick it off each day.*

✅ Action Step

Use the Smart Savings Tracker (included after this page) to:

- Choose your **first savings goal**

- Pick your **saving method** (or mix and match)

- Track your progress visually or use your own style

🖊 **My savings goal is:** $_____
🖊 **Target date to reach it:** _____
🖊 **Saving method I'm trying:**

- ☐ Daily saves
- ☐ Round-ups
- ☐ Auto-transfer
- ☐ Challenges
- ☐ Combo

💸 Smart Savings Tracker Worksheet

Use this worksheet to track your progress toward your savings goal. Choose a method (or two), set your target, and record each contribution as you go. Watching your progress grow is one of the best motivators to keep going!

Savings Goal: _____

Target Amount ($): _____

Start Date: _____

Target End Date: _____

Method(s): □ Daily saves □ Round-ups □ Auto-transfer □ Challenges □ Combo

Date	Amount ($)	Method	Notes

⭐

You've Got This!

You're building a safety net!

Every dollar saved is a little more peace of mind. Even the small amounts matter.

You're showing up for future you 💚

📈 Module 6: Beginner Wealth

You don't need $10k to start; just $5 and a plan.

📘 Why This Matters

Most people believe wealth is something that happens *later*, after you earn more, pay off everything, or "get lucky." But here's the truth: wealth isn't about a big windfall. It's about **consistency over time**. Starting small, starting now, and building habits that grow.

When you begin investing (even with just $5) you start to shift your identity. You're no longer just trying to survive financially. You're building something. You're thinking long-term. That mindset shift is as powerful as the dollars themselves.

The earlier you start, the more time is on your side and time is the most valuable tool you have.

Wealth is not about luck or income level. It's about small, smart steps repeated over time.

✨ What You'll Learn

- How compound interest works (and why it's magical)

- What superannuation is and how to make the most of it

- Micro-investing apps for beginners

- What "wealth" actually means (hint: it's not just money)

IMPORTANT NOTE:

The information on the following pages should be discussed with a **Financial Planner or Financial Advisor**. They are experts in superannuation, investing and wealth management. Always consult a professional before making any changes to your superannuation or when you begin investing.

🧙 The Magic of Compound Interest

Small amounts + time = big results

Compound interest is often called the *eighth wonder of the world* (and for good reason!) It's the process where your money not only earns returns, but then those returns start earning returns too. Over time, this creates a **snowball effect** that can turn even the smallest savings into significant wealth.

Here's the formula behind it:

Money + Time + Consistency = Growth

Let's see this in action:

> 💬 **Example 1:** You invest $10 a week ($43.30 per month on average) into a simple high-interest savings account with an interest rate of 4.99% per year, compounded monthly.

📊 **Monthly Compound Savings Breakdown**

Month	Contribution ($)	Int. Earned ($)	End Balance ($)
1	$43.30	$0.18	$43.48
2	$43.30	$0.36	$87.14
3	$43.30	$0.54	$130.99
4	$43.30	$0.91	$175.01
...	...	...	...
60 (5 years)	$43.30	$6.42	$2944.66

By Month 60 (5 years), you've contributed a total of $2,598 and earned **$346.66** in interest. All off saving just $10 a week!

Imagine what it could be if you saved more than $10 a week.

Example 2: You start with a one-time $2000 investment in a managed fund through an investment app that averages 7% return on your investment.

At 7% annual growth:

- After 10 years: Approx. $3,934
- After 20 years: Approx. $7,739
- After 30 years: Approx. **$15,225!**
  (That's more than **7x your original money**, without adding another cent!)

But don't be fooled. Growth in investing isn't guaranteed. The share market could crash, or a financial institution could go bankrupt; there are several ways that you could lose money. That's why it's important to speak to an expert; *Financial Planners and Financial Advisors* are an invaluable resource that will help you on your investing journey.

⏰ Why Starting Early Matters

Time is your secret weapon.

A person who starts saving at age 25 and invests $20/week until age 35 (just 10 years) and then stops, will often end up with more money than someone who waits until age 35 and invests $20/week until age 65. That's the power of compounding and time working together.

"Compound interest is the most powerful force in the universe." – (Often attributed to Einstein... and repeated by just about every financial educator since!)

Also bear in mind that the so-called secret of "timing the market" is completely false. The real winner is time IN the market. The longer your money stays invested, the more chance it has to grow, even if you're only contributing small amounts.

✅ Action Step

What's one amount you could commit to investing weekly (even just $5 or $10) knowing it could grow with time?

🖊 *Write down your number and your commitment*

Amount: $_____

Frequency: ☐ Weekly ☐ Fortnightly ☐ Monthly

Method: ☐ Auto-transfer ☐ App ☐ Manual top-up

🏛️ Understanding Superannuation

Your future wealth is already growing, so let's make sure it's working for you.

Superannuation (or "super") is money set aside by your employer throughout your working life to help fund your retirement. It's **compulsory**, it's **invested**, and over time it may become your **largest financial asset**.

But here's the thing: most people ignore it until it's too late to make a big difference. By simply paying attention now (even if you're not contributing extra) you could **gain tens of thousands of dollars more** over your lifetime.

📚 What You Should Know About Your Super

1. Your Fund Type & Investment Option

Most super funds let you choose how your money is invested. The options usually include:

- **Growth** – Higher risk, higher potential return. Good for long timelines (i.e. if you're younger and still have many working years ahead of you).

- **Balanced** – Mix of growth and defensive investments. Moderate risk.

- **Conservative** – Lower risk, lower return. Safer but grows slower.

💡 Tip

If you're decades away from retirement, a growth option may suit your long-term goals. It's worth speaking to a Financial Planner or Financial Advisor to find out more!

2. Fees Matter… A Lot

Some super funds charge much higher fees than others. Over 30 years, **high fees can eat up tens of thousands of dollars** from your balance.

🔍 *Check your fund's annual admin and investment fees.*

Even a difference of 0.5% adds up significantly over time.

3. Insurance You May Be Paying For

Your super might include:

- Life insurance

- Total and permanent disability (TPD)

- Income protection

These can be valuable, but if you have multiple funds, you might be **paying duplicate fees** for insurance you don't need.

📋 If you have more than one fund, you could consider consolidating to avoid paying extra fees or having multiple insurance policies that you're paying for too.

But when playing around with super, it's always a good idea to first consult a **Financial Planner or Financial Advisor**. They're *the experts you need* to succeed.

🚀 Optional Power Move

If you're in a position to do so, **voluntary contributions** to super (also called *after-tax contributions* or *salary sacrifice*) can significantly boost your retirement nest egg and may even save you on tax now.

But, again, whenever you're messing with super you absolutely should consult a **Financial Planner or Financial Advisor** first. They know their stuff and won't steer you wrong.

✅ Action Step

Log in to your super account (or app) and find the following:

✅ Check	Notes
What's your current balance?	$_____
What investment option are you in?	☐ Growth ☐ Balanced ☐ Conservative ☐ Not Sure
What are your annual fees?	$_____
Do you have insurance cover?	☐ Yes ☐ No ☐ Not Sure
Are you with more than one fund?	☐ Yes ☐ No

📱 Micro-Investing for Beginners

Small amounts, smart tools; investing has never been more accessible.

Once upon a time, investing in the stock market meant needing thousands of dollars, a financial advisor, and a fair bit of paperwork. But not anymore.

Micro-investing apps now make it simple for *everyday Australians* to get started with as little as $1, all from your phone.

🧩 What Is Micro-Investing?

Micro-investing is a simple, beginner-friendly way to start investing with just a little bit of money (known as *capital*), sometimes even just **$5**. Micro-investing let you dip your toes in with spare change or small transfers.

Think of micro-investing like putting your leftover coins in a jar, but smarter. Because even though those coins in a jar are worth something, but they're not *working* for you.

Some apps round up your everyday purchases to the nearest dollar and invest the difference. For example, if you buy a coffee for $3.60, the app might round it up to $4 and invest that **40 cents**. It's automatic and painless.

Just like round-ups for savings from Module 5, it adds up quickly without you even noticing. The difference here is that the small amounts invested then start working for you. And while the returns may seem small to begin with, they can **compound** over time. And we all know *compounding is magic!*

Platforms also let you set up **regular small transfers**, like $5 or $10 a week, into a professionally managed investment fund. Over time, those small amounts **add up**, and your money starts working for you behind the scenes.

📱 How Does It Work?

You don't need to research individual stocks or understand the share market; the app does all the heavy lifting.

- You download a micro-investing app

- You connect your bank account

- You choose how much and how often to invest (e.g. round-ups, weekly transfers, or one-off deposits)

- The app automatically invests your money into a **diversified fund**, such as shares, ETFs, or ethical portfolios, based on your tolerance to risk and your overall goals.

It's **passive, low-effort, and beginner-friendly**.

This is a game changer for many Aussies wanting to join the investing gig.

- You can **start small**, which removes the biggest barrier to entry.

- You build the **habit** of investing early, without waiting until you "earn more."

- You learn as you go, and see how your money can grow over time.

However, don't just take my word for it. Do your research if investing is something you want to dip your toe into, and **please please PLEASE**; go see a **Financial Planner or Financial Advisor** before making any big changes.

I cannot stress this enough; <u>they are the experts</u>.

✅ Action Step

It's time to look at some tools that may work for you, and that starts with a little research.

Use the space on the next page to research and compare some **Australian micro-investing platforms**. Look for ones that align with your comfort level, investment goals, and lifestyle. Many platforms have helpful videos, FAQs, and beginner guides right on their websites.

🔍 Where to Look:

- Start by searching: "**Best micro-investing apps Australia**"
- Visit the official websites of apps, especially their FAQ sections
- Use comparison sites to see comparisons of fees and ratings
- Check for reviews from reputable sources

💡 Tip

Don't aim for "perfect." Aim for *progress*. You can always change platforms later. What matters now is getting started.

📋 Your Comparison Notes

Platform Name	Min $ to Start	Fees	Key Features	Would You Use It?
				☐ Yes ☐ No
				☐ Yes ☐ No
				☐ Yes ☐ No
				☐ Yes ☐ No

💡 Tip

Micro-investing is about **building the habit**. Don't stress about returns right now. Focus on getting used to seeing yourself as *someone who invests.*

$5 here, $10 there. It's about *behaviour*, not big bucks.

🌱 What Wealth Really Means

It's not just about money. It's about freedom, peace, and choice.

Most people define wealth in numbers: how much is in the bank, what kind of house you live in, or how early you can retire. But those numbers don't tell the full story. **Wealth is more than financial.** It's about building a life that feels secure, spacious, and aligned with your values.

🏝️ True Wealth Looks Like...

- Having **enough saved** that an unexpected bill doesn't shake you

- Feeling **confident and in control** of where your money is going

- Knowing you could **take a break** from work if needed

- Having the **freedom to say no** to things that don't serve you

- Being able to say yes to holidays, generosity, rest, and joy

Wealth is **options**. It's **breathing room**. It's not about being rich, it's about being *well-resourced*.

> 💬 **Example**
>
> For Mia, wealth means being able to buy school uniforms **without panic**.
>
> For Dylan, it's *finally* going part-time to spend more time with his family.

For you, it might be something completely different. And that's the point.

✏️ Journal Prompt

What does wealth mean to you today, in your real life?

Write down what "being wealthy" looks like to you, not in numbers, but in feelings, time, freedom, or peace of mind.

📘 *I'll know I'm wealthy when I can...*

_____

_____

_____

_____

By redefining wealth in personal terms, you start making money decisions that are aligned with *your* version of success, not someone else's.

This is where budgeting, saving, and investing all start to feel *worth it*.

⭐

You've Got This!

You've started building wealth. Not "one day", but right now! That's a massive shift.

It's happening. And it's yours.

📅 Module 7: Your Strategy Game Plan

Tie it all together: Your personalized roadmap.

📘 Why This Matters

You've already done the heavy lifting: you faced the numbers, shifted your mindset, and made real moves toward budgeting, saving, and building wealth.

Now it's time to lock in.

The last 30 days were about **momentum**, not perfection. This is the time where you reinforce your new money habits with a simple, personalised plan; one that keeps you feeling motivated, in control, and encouraged as you move forward.

Consistency now builds confidence later.

✨ What You'll Learn

- How to review your progress

- What habits to keep and which to let go of

- How to reward yourself without spending

- The power of small accountability tricks

✅ How to Review Your Progress

Progress isn't just about numbers, it's about awareness, confidence, and small wins that build lasting change. Before you move forward, take time to look back. What worked? What didn't? What felt better than before?

Even if your budget wasn't perfect or you didn't hit every goal, you've already built more clarity and control than you had 30 days ago. That's real progress.

✨ Reflection Prompts

Use these questions to help guide your review:

- What's one money win I'm proud of this month?

- What habit or tool helped me feel more in control?

- Where did I feel stuck, overwhelmed, or avoidant, and what might help next time?

💬 Example

I saved $150 without really trying just by automating it. That felt like a huge win. I still overspent on takeaway in Week 2, but now I can see it clearly and make a plan for it.

👆 What Habits to Keep (and Which to Tweak)

A money strategy isn't about being perfect, it's about experimenting. Now that you've tested new habits, let's figure out what's *actually working for you*... and what needs adjusting.

✊ Keep the habits that help you:

- Feel more **in control** of your money

- Reduce **stress or guesswork**

- Align your spending with your **values and priorities**

Example:

✓ You started reviewing your bank balance every morning with your coffee and it made you feel calm and prepared. That's a keeper.

✓ You used a visual tracker for debt or savings, and it kept you motivated. Stick with it!

🔧 Tweak or drop habits that:

- Feel **confusing, stressful, or forced**

- You keep skipping or dreading

- Don't seem to move the needle for *your* goals

Example:

✗ You tried using a budgeting app but found yourself ignoring it after a week. Maybe a simple weekly check-in would be better?

✗ You restricted all your "fun" spending and ended up binge spending. Time to try a **Play Money** approach instead.

✅ Action Step

Split your habits into the two columns below to decide what to keep and what to tweak.

KEEP THIS 👏	TWEAK THIS 🔧
(e.g. Weekly budget review)	(e.g. Daily app check-in. Let's try paper instead. The app makes me feel anxious)

💡 Tip

Start by keeping just 2 - 3 core habits that feel strong, and tweak 1 - 2 that need adjusting or scrapping.

Sustainable change is better than perfect plans.

🎉 Celebrate Without the Spend

Changing your money habits takes effort, and effort deserves recognition. But here's the trick: rewarding yourself **doesn't have to mean spending money**. In fact, non-financial rewards can feel even more meaningful, especially when they align with what actually fills your cup.

Let's celebrate your wins without undoing your progress.

💡 Reward Ideas That Cost Nothing (But Feel Amazing)

📺 A guilt-free binge night of your favourite show

🛁 A long bath with a podcast and no interruptions

🌳 A solo walk or day in nature

📚 A quiet afternoon reading or journaling

🎧 Creating a playlist that marks this moment

💤 Sleeping in or taking an intentional nap

🧠 A deep catch-up session with a friend

✅ The joy of checking something off your bucket list (that doesn't cost money)

💬 Example

After I hit my first savings goal, I booked out a whole Sunday just for me. No errands, no guilt. I slept in, made pancakes, and binge watched Buffy the Vampire Slayer. It was awesome!

✅ Action Step

Pick rewards that will feel like a *real treat* to you. Write them down and assign them to milestones. E.g. completing your 5-Day Savings Challenge, sticking to your budget 3 weeks in a row, or a big one; paying off your first debt.

📅 Milestone	🎁 Free Reward
(e.g. Sticking to my budget for 3 weeks in a row)	(e.g. Making my favourite snack and watching my favourite movie)

💡 Tip

Celebrating builds momentum. You're not just managing money; you're becoming someone who follows through. So, celebrate every milestone, every small win, and you'll become **consistent and intentional** with your money.

🔗 Tiny Tricks, Big Wins: The Power of Accountability

Let's be honest, staying consistent with money habits isn't always about knowledge or motivation. It's about **follow-through**. That's where accountability comes in. You don't need a coach or a bootcamp; just a few small systems that remind you to keep showing up.

When you know someone (or something) will notice if you check in, you're more likely to stick with your goals. This isn't about pressure or guilt; it's about creating gentle nudges that keep you on track, even when life gets busy.

📌 Try These Simple Accountability Tools

- **The Weekly Review Ritual**: Pick a time each week (e.g. Sunday morning) to check your budget, savings, and spending. Pair it with a treat like your favourite coffee and French toast.

- **Budget Buddy System**: Team up with a friend who's also working on their finances. Set a day or time to text each other weekly wins and stumbles.

- **Habit Trackers or Calendars**: Use a printable tracker or calendar to physically tick off the days you followed your plan. Visual progress is powerful.

- **Auto-Reminders**: Set calendar events or app notifications to review your money every 7 days.

   ### 💬 Example

   I set a 10-minute calendar event every Friday morning called 'Money Strategy.' I just glance at my bank account, write one win and one challenge in my notes app, and move on. That tiny routine keeps me grounded.

✅ Action Step

Think about what keeps you on track in other areas of your life and write down 2 – 3 ideas you could try to keep yourself accountable.

_____

_____

_____

_____

_____

_____

_____

_____

💡 Tip

The goal isn't perfection. It's showing up regularly enough that your habits become automatic. One small nudge at the right time can change everything.

📋 Your Strategy Game Plan

Here is your **From Money Stress to Money Strategy Game Plan** to help you work through all 7 core modules and 3 bonus sections in one month, without overwhelm. This plan is structured to give you regular wins, reflection time, and manageable weekly focus areas.

📆 Week 1: Get Grounded & Gain Clarity

Day 1:

🧠 *Module 1: Your Money Mindset*

> ➢ Reflect on your past experiences with money. Complete the mindset prompts.
> ➢ Journal your new money story.

Day 2:

📸 *Module 2: The Snapshot*

> ➢ Fill out your Snapshot Worksheet.
> ➢ Bonus: Track your subscriptions and debts with the provided trackers.

Day 3:

🎁 *Bonus 1: Quick Wins Toolkit*

> ➢ Choose at least 2 quick wins and complete them today.

Day 4:

💰 *Module 3: The 2-Hour Budget Reset*

> ➢ Set up your real-life baseline budget. Use the template and follow the steps.
> ➢ Schedule a review time in two weeks.

Day 5:

🎁 *Bonus 2: Emotional Spending SOS*

➢ Explore your triggers and reset strategies.

Day 6-7:

✨ *Catch-up & Reflect*

➢ Revisit anything you missed.
➢ Reflect: What surprised you most this week?

📅 Week 2: Reset Spending & Build Momentum

Day 8:

🐿 *Module 4: Debt Demolition*

➢ Complete your Debt Snapshot Worksheet.
➢ Choose a payoff method and make one progress action (e.g. request a better rate).

Day 9-10:

🎁 *Bonus 3: Money Confidence Scripts*

➢ Choose one script to rehearse or journal — start with a provider or housemate script.
➢ Try a Money Confidence Script with one provider and ask for a discount.

Day 11:

🎓 *Module 5: Smart Savings*

➢ Pick a method and start your savings goal with the tracker.
➢ Try a 10-day mini challenge or set up an automatic transfer.

Day 12-13:

✏️ Check in with your budget and spending.

- ➢ Have your habits shifted?
- ➢ What feels easier or harder?

Day 14:

✅ *Mini Review*

- ➢ Where have you gained momentum?
- ➢ What's one small win you want to celebrate?

📅 Week 3: Start Building Wealth

Day 15-18:

📈 *Module 6: Beginner Wealth*

- ➢ Learn how compound interest works.
- ➢ Check your super balance.
- ➢ Choose an ethical investing article or video and reflect in your journal.
- ➢ Research micro-investing apps or platforms. Compare features like fees, automation, and ethical options.
- ➢ *Optional:* Invest your first $5–$10.

Day 19:

🔍 *Reflection*

- ➢ What does wealth mean to you now?
- ➢ Write down your definition in your workbook.

Day 20-21:

✅ *Mid-point Review*

> ➢ Revisit your budget and savings progress.
> ➢ What needs tweaking?

📅 Week 4: Strategy & Next Steps

Day 22:

📅 *Module 7: Your Strategy Game Plan*

> ➢ Review your journey so far.
> ➢ Identify what habits worked and what didn't.

Day 23:

> ➢ Choose 3 rewards and a check-in method.

Day 24-25:

> ➢ Reflect on how your money mindset has shifted.
> ➢ Write a letter to your future self, 30 days from now.

Day 26:

🎁 *Revisit Bonus 1-3*

> ➢ Apply another quick win.
> ➢ Rehearse a money confidence script again.
> ➢ Optional: Journal about your emotional spending patterns and how they've changed.

Day 27–28:

> ➢ Share your progress with someone you trust, a budgeting buddy, friend or partner.

Day 29:

✅ *Final Review*

- ➤ Look back at your original Snapshot and see how far you've come.
- ➤ Circle 3 wins you're proud of.

Day 30:

🎉 *Celebrate!*

- ➤ Do something free or low-cost that makes you feel *rich in life*.
- ➤ Remember: you've created a strategy, not just a one-off fix.

🔐 Your Commitment to Your Strategy

Now that you have gone through the strategy, it's time to commit to it.

1. Choose your check-in/accountability system

☐ Weekly reflection journal

☐ Budgeting buddy (name: _____)

☐ Sunday planner session

☐ Other: _____

2. Pick 1 - 2 small habits to commit to

Example: "Log in to my savings account every Friday and transfer $10."

Example: "Review my spending on Sundays."

✎ _____

✎ _____

3. Choose 3 non-spending rewards

✎ _____

✎ _____

✎ _____

📝 Journal Prompt

Take 5 - 10 minutes to free-write your thoughts below.

What surprised you about this process? What are you learning about yourself as a person? What would you like to carry forward?

💡 Tip

There are no wrong answers.

_____
_____
_____
_____
_____
_____
_____
_____
_____
_____
_____
_____
_____
_____
_____
_____
_____
_____
_____

⭐

You've Got This!

You didn't just survive this process; you **reset your money mindset**, built systems that actually work, and proved you can do this.

You are not "bad with money."

You're someone who's *learning*, *growing*, and *making real change* happen.

This is just the beginning.

🎁 Bonus 1: The Quick Wins Toolkit

Instant wins to save you money TODAY!

📘 Why This Matters

When you're just getting started, it can feel like change takes forever. But small, fast wins are the spark that builds motivation. They give you visible progress right away and remind you that **you're in control**.

Even a few dollars saved today proves that your effort works. And once you see results, you're more likely to keep going. Quick wins aren't about penny-pinching; they're about **taking smart, confident action**.

✨ What You'll Learn

- How to find and cancel unused subscriptions

- How to negotiate your bills

- Simple ways to reduce your grocery and utility costs

- Easy tricks to free up money without stress or sacrifice

💸 Find and Cancel Unused Subscriptions

In the age of auto-renewals and free trials that quietly become monthly charges, it's surprisingly easy to lose track of what you're actually paying for. That $7.99 music app or $13.99 streaming service might seem small but if you're not using it, it's money out the door for nothing.

Even worse, most subscriptions fly under the radar until your bank account feels lighter than expected. Identifying and cutting out just *two or three unused services* can free up $20 - 50+ per month instantly.

🔍 How to Find Them:

- **Check your bank and PayPal transactions** for the past 30–90 days. Look for:
    - Apple, Google, Spotify, Netflix, Amazon, Calm, Duolingo, etc., anything that seems to repeat.

- **Search your email** for "receipt," "subscription," "auto-renew," or "thank you for your purchase." This will highlight what subscriptions you may have forgotten about.

- There are free tools (apps, programs, etc.) that can scan for recurring payments, but you can also do this manually with a pen and paper.

✂️ Cancel Like a Pro:

- Go into your device's settings or directly to the provider's website to cancel.

- If you can't cancel immediately, **set a calendar reminder** the day before it renews.

- Screenshot the cancellation confirmation for your records.

··· **My Personal Example**:

I am a TV junky. I'll admit that. Please don't judge me.

I can spend an entire day just sitting on the couch, watching movie after movie and not bat an eye. Personally, I consider that a wonderful day at home.

So, you can imagine that I love the streaming services, not just the paid ones but the freebies with ads too. **And you'd be right!**

Well one payday I was doing my bills (I use a hybrid of Zero-Based and Account-Based Budgeting from module 3) and I noticed that I was spending more than $150 per month just to watch TV.

And that wasn't including the random $5 - $10 every now and then to rent digital movies and shows!

That's almost **$2000** every year!

I knew I had to change. Not only was I spending a huge amount of my hard-earned money on something that I couldn't even own at the end of the day, I realised that I was only using 1 – 2 services. I hadn't logged into Netflix or Prime or Binge for months; **but I sure was paying for them!**

So, crunch time came; I sat down, searched for, and found every single subscription service I was paying for (and there were *so many*!), and chose which to keep and which to cull. The cancellation process was simple for most subscriptions, and it took about an hour when it was all said and done.

And now, I use a rotating system for streaming services. I'll subscribe to a service for a month or two, depending on what I want to watch, and then cancel it and subscribe to the next service.

I'm still a TV junky, but I have a lot more money back in my pocket…

… for snacks 🍫

🧠 "Is It Worth It?" A 3-Question Filter

To help you in deciding what to keep and what to cull, ask yourself these three questions:

1. **Do I actually use this?**
    Be honest. When was the last time you watched, listened, read, or logged in? If it's been over a month and you didn't miss it, that's a clear sign.

2. **Does it bring consistent value?**
    Some subscriptions might be used occasionally, but still worth keeping if they genuinely improve your life. Like a music app for daily commutes, or a business tool that saves you hours.

3. **Could I pause or downgrade it?**
    Many platforms let you pause for 1 - 3 months or switch to a cheaper plan. That way, you're not locked in, but you can always come back when it makes sense.

💡 Tip

If you're not sure yet, cancel anyway. If you truly miss it, you'll know; you can always re-subscribe later.

✅ Action Step

List the subscriptions you've found, and mark which ones you're keeping or cancelling:

Subscription	Monthly Cost	Keep or Cancel?	Date Cancelled
E.g. *Netflix*	*$16.99*	*Cancel*	*March 2*
E.g. *Spotify*	*$17.99*	*Keep*	*—*

📰 Negotiate Your Bills Like a Boss

Yes, even if you hate phone calls.

Most companies expect you to call and ask for a better deal, they just don't advertise it. Telcos, electricity providers, even insurance companies *often have discounts*, promotional rates, or hardship options available. But here's the secret: **they rarely offer them unless you ask**.

A 10-minute call could save you hundreds a year. And you don't need to be pushy; you just need a simple script and the confidence to ask.

📞 What Can You Negotiate?

- **Internet** & **phone bills**

- **Electricity** & **gas rates**

- **Insurance premiums** (home, car, contents)

- **Credit card interest** or annual fees

- Even **buy now, pay later** or loan repayments during hardship

📝 What to Do Before You Call

1. **Grab your latest bill** (or log into your online account).

2. **Check the competitor's pricing** even just a quick Google search can reveal a better deal.

3. **Know what you're asking for**: a lower price, fees waived, hardship support, or payment extensions; most companies want to keep your business, so they'll do what *you need* to keep your business.

🗣 Sample Script (Edit it to Suit Your Style)

"Hi, I've been reviewing my bills and trying to cut back on expenses. I've seen some lower rates elsewhere and wanted to know if you could offer me a better deal or any discounts for loyal customers?"

If you're struggling financially, try:

"I'm currently experiencing financial stress and trying to get on top of things. Do you have any payment support, hardship programs, or ways to lower my bill?"

💡 Tip

Be polite but confident. If the first person can't help, ask: *"Is there someone else I can speak to about this?"*

IMPORTANT NOTE:

If you are experiencing financial hardship, Financial Counsellors are available in every Australian state and territory, and they are 100% free.

Financial Counsellors can help people struggling with debt and money issues by assessing the situation, creating budgets, negotiating with creditors on your behalf (with your permission of course), and more. They don't give financial advice but instead empower you to manage bills, fines, mortgage stress, and credit card debt. All 100% free and confidential.

You can find a Financial Counsellor by doing a simple Google search for Financial Counsellors in your local area, call the National Debt Helpline on 1800 007 007 or use their website (www.ndh.org.au) to find local services.

You are not alone.

✅ Action Step

List some of your service providers that you could contact and then *make that call!*

Provider	What You Asked For	Result	Notes
E.g. *Optus Internet*	*Lower monthly rate*	*$20/month discount for 6 months*	*Easy win!*
E.g. *AAMI Insurance*	*Fee waiver or discount*	*Offered $50 loyalty credit*	*Renewing next month*

💡 Tip

Even **one call a week** can build real momentum. Treat it like a money win, because it is!

🛒 Shop Your Kitchen Before You Shop the Store

It sounds simple, but checking your pantry, fridge, and freezer before heading to the shops can be a total money-saver *and* a meal-planning game changer.

We often buy more of what we already have (hello, three bags of rice!) or miss out on easy meals we could've made at home. Doing a quick check helps you **avoid duplicates**, **reduce food waste**, and **stretch your grocery budget** without sacrificing good food.

🔍 How to Do a Pantry Check in 5 Minutes:

- Open the fridge, pantry, and freezer.

- Write down 2 - 3 meal ideas based on what you already have.

    E.g. Pasta + tuna + tinned tomatoes = tuna pasta bake.

- Take a photo of your shelves if you tend to forget what's there.

💡 Tip

You can quickly and easily work out what meals you can make based on what you already have by putting your fridge, pantry and freezer items into an AI chat and asking for recipes using *only* those ingredients.

The AI can come up with some very tasty options and you're not spending a cent!

Win, win!

🔌 Cut Costs Without the Call: Simple Utility Hacks That Work

Reducing your utility bills doesn't always require negotiation. Sometimes, all it takes is a few small changes at home. These no-contact strategies are quick to action, low-effort, and can deliver real savings on **electricity**, **gas**, and **water** over time.

⚡ Energy-Saving Wins

- **Switch off at the wall**: Appliances on standby can account for up to 10% of your power bill. Turn off devices like TVs, consoles, microwaves, and chargers at the wall when not in use. And if you're going away for a weekend or longer, think about cleaning out your fridge and switching it off too.

- **Swap to LED bulbs**: They use about 75% less energy and last 5 - 10x longer. Even replacing one or two high-use lights can cut costs. The same can be said for smart lights. While standard LEDs are already efficient, smart features like scheduling and remote control provide extra savings by preventing energy waste from forgotten lights, with the potential to reduce usage by 20 - 30% more.

- **Use power-hungry appliances at off-peak times** (if you're on time-of-use pricing): Think dishwashers, washing machines, and dryers, and commit to using them after 8pm or on weekends. Just be sure to check your electricity bill and find out your off-peak times.

- **Get a solar powered clothes dryer:** Yes, I mean using the greatest resource Australia has all year round; the Sun. Drying your washing on a clothesline instead of in a dryer can save big money, and there's no chance of shrinkage. Plus, it's a 100% free resource!

🛁 Hot Water = Hidden Expense

- **Take shorter showers**: Reducing your shower by just 2 minutes could save hundreds of litres of hot water each week. Or, if you're really brave, try a cold shower. It's great in summer to cool down and has the added benefit of less hot water usage.

- **Use cold water for laundry**: Most loads don't need hot water. About the only time you really need hot water is if you need intense stain/grease removal, or you're sanitising items such as pet bedding. Switch to cold for instant savings on energy and watch your expenses drop.

- **Fix dripping taps**: A single slow leak can waste thousands of litres per year. And if you're paying for water usage, that's a lot of wasted dollars! Be sure to check your bathrooms and kitchens regularly, as well as your toilet cistern. If it's constantly running, you're literally flushing money down the toilet!

🌡️ Heating & Cooling Efficiency

- **Close doors and curtains**: Contain warmth in winter and block out heat in summer by closing off rooms and curtains to reduce heater or AC use.

- **Use a fan first**: Fans are far cheaper to run than heaters or air conditioners. Even in colder months, a reverse fan can help circulate warm air from up at your roof level. Remember primary school science?

- **Dress for the weather**: Layer up before cranking the heat. A cosy hoodie or blanket with sleeves (if you know, you know) is cheaper than an extra hour of electric heating.

Water-Saving Tweaks

- **Only run full loads**: Whether it's dishes or laundry, full loads are the most efficient way to use water and energy. For laundry, pick 1 day per week to do all your washing (clothes, towels, bedding, etc.) to save having to do multiple small loads during the week. As for your dishwasher, if you don't have at least half a load, fill up that sink, do it the old-fashioned way, and put on a podcast to really make use of your time.

- **Install a water-saving showerhead:** Water-saving showerheads can be inexpensive and do a great deal to decrease your consumption. Just be sure it's removable if you're renting or get your landlords permission if you're wanting to install a permanent one. I honestly don't think they'll say no to the upgrade!

- **Water plants with cooking water**: Let boiled veggie water cool and use it to hydrate your garden or pot plants. Not only are your plants getting the water they need, but they're also getting nutrients from your veggies. You'll have healthier plants and you'll be using your resources wisely.

Journal Prompt

What are some simple changes you can make in your household?

💸 Find Hidden Cash Without Feeling the Pinch

Free up funds without giving up everything you love.

Saving money doesn't always mean cutting out joy or living on the edge of burnout. Sometimes, all it takes is shifting habits, reframing choices, or catching leaks in your everyday spending.

These simple, stress-free swaps can help you **unlock extra cash** without sacrificing what matters most.

🧠 Mindful Spending Tweaks

- **Delay non-urgent purchases**: Add the item you want it to a 30-day list instead of buying straight away. Most impulse buys fade in a week, and you'll spend less without even noticing.

  ✅ **Action:** Create a note on your phone titled "30-Day List" and add one item to it instead of buying it. Then set a reminder in your phone to look at the list in 30 days. Do you still want it?

- **Review your "little leaks"**: These are low-cost habits that sneak under the radar like daily bottled drinks, unused apps, $2 ATM fees, etc. Identify just *one* to pause or replace.

  ✅ **Action:** Bring your own water bottle instead of buying one at the servo = **$3/day saved**. And if you're doing that every day, that's **$21/week**, **$84/month**, or **$1008/year**! That could be a huge boost to your emergency fund.

🎯 Swaps That Don't Feel Like Sacrifices

Instead of this...	Try this...	Est. Weekly Savings
Takeaway lunch x3/week	Meal prep 2 days + 1 café treat day	$30 - 40
Subscriptions you barely use	Cancel or pause for 1 – 2 months	$10+
Buying books/magazines	Use your local library (they even have eBooks now!)	$10 - 25
The gym you don't go to	YouTube workouts or community walking groups	$15 - 20

These little swaps can make a big impact. All up, if you made all of these changes, you'd be saving $65 – 95 per week!

📦 Inventory = Instant Budget Boost

Before you buy anything new, *check what you already have*.

- Food in the pantry

- Toiletries in the cupboard

- Items you forgot you owned (e.g. clothes, electronics, etc.)

This "use what you have" approach can free a ton spending without feeling like a chore.

Also, if you forgot you owned it (clothes, electronics, gadgets), do you really need it? If not, sell it! You get rid of clutter while making **extra cash**!

✅ Action Step

Tiny actions. Real money wins. Get momentum fast.

Choose at least **2 quick wins** from the list below to complete today. You can always come back and check off more later. Every small action adds up to big change over time.

Quick Win Action	Date Completed	Notes or Outcome
☐ Cancel a subscription you haven't used in the last 30 days	___/___/_____	*(e.g. Saved $13/month on streaming)*
☐ Use the bill negotiation script to call your internet or energy provider	___/___/_____	*(e.g. Got $120 credit applied!)*
☐ Do a pantry check before grocery shopping	___/___/_____	*(e.g. Planned 3 meals from what we had)*
☐ Swap one weekly purchase for a DIY version (energy drink, takeaway)	___/___/_____	*(e.g. Made iced coffee at home)*
☐ Do one "use what I have" inventory check (food, toiletries, wardrobe)	___/___/_____	*(e.g. Found 2 unused shampoo bottles!)*
☐ Move one item to your "Think List" instead of impulse buying	___/___/_____	*(e.g. Decided to wait on new headphones)*
☐ Reduce one "little leak" (ATM fee, bottled drink habit)	___/___/_____	*(e.g. Switched to BYO bottle)*

⭐

You've Got This!

You've proven that you can take quick, powerful action. These aren't just money-saving moves; they're *identity-building steps*.

You're becoming someone who takes charge of their finances.

Keep stacking those wins!

🎁 Bonus 2: Emotional Spending SOS

Reset after a splurge, without guilt.

📘 Why This Matters

Emotional spending is incredibly common and totally human. Whether it's a bad day, a celebration, or a moment of boredom, we often spend money to feel better. But this bonus module isn't about guilt or perfection. It's about building awareness, self-compassion, and practical strategies that help you hit pause instead of spiral.

Understanding your emotional spending patterns is a powerful tool. Once you can name the trigger, you can start choosing a different response; one that feels just as comforting but *doesn't* sabotage your financial goals.

✨ What You'll Learn

- How to spot emotional spending triggers

- What to do immediately after a "whoops" moment

- How to build compassion and "guardrails" for next time

🔍 How to Spot Emotional Spending (Before It Happens)

Emotional spending isn't always obvious in the moment. It can feel like a perfectly reasonable decision, until the guilt or regret creeps in afterward. The key to breaking the cycle is learning how to notice the early signs *before* the purchase happens.

Here's how to build that awareness:

1. Know Your Personal Triggers

Emotional spending usually starts with a feeling, not a financial need. Some of the most common triggers include:

- **Stress or overwhelm** → "I deserve a treat."

- **Boredom** → "I'll just browse…"

- **Loneliness or sadness** → "This will cheer me up."

- **Celebration** → "I earned this."

- **Insecurity or comparison** → "Everyone else has one."

📝 Journal Prompt

Think about the last time you bought something you didn't plan to.

What was going on in your day (or in your head) before that?

_____

_____

_____

_____

2. Spot the Patterns

You're more likely to spend impulsively in certain situations. These patterns are unique to *you*, and once you spot them, you can start preparing for them.

✅ **Examples of common emotional spending patterns**

- Late-night online shopping when you're tired or stressed

- Grabbing takeaway after a long day instead of cooking

- Clicking "add to cart" after scrolling social media

- "Just looking" turns into a checkout when you're bored at work

Use a journal or notes app to jot down when these moments happen; not to judge, but to observe. Awareness is step one.

Journal Prompt

Think about the last few times you bought things that weren't actually necessary.

Can you see any patterns that happen at those times?

_____

_____

_____

_____

3. Identify the *Need Behind the Spend*

Every emotional spend is trying to meet a need, for comfort, excitement, connection, or control. The trick is learning to name that need *before* spending.

Ask yourself:

- Am I feeling a strong emotion right now?

- Would I still want this tomorrow?

- What else might meet this need that doesn't involve spending?

Journal Prompt

Think about the last time you bought something you didn't plan to.

Can you identify what you were feeling/need when you made the purchase?

_____

_____

_____

_____

✅ Action Step: Create Your Personal Trigger Map

On the following page draw a circle in the middle and write **"Spending Triggers"** in the centre.

Around the circle, list all the emotions, situations, or patterns you notice in yourself.

Examples

- Feeling left out after seeing others on social media

- Rewarding myself after finishing a stressful task

- Lonely Sunday afternoons

The next time you feel the urge to spend, check your trigger map first. Is this one of your patterns showing up?

🩺 The "Whoops" Recovery Plan

Let's reset after an impulse spend, without spiralling.

We've all been there: one click, one swipe, one "I'll deal with it later" moment and boom, you've spent money you didn't plan to. Maybe it's a latte, maybe it's a $200 Amazon haul. Either way, that sinking feeling hits.

But here's the truth: **this is just a moment, not a failure.**

You haven't ruined your budget, broken your progress, or "blown it." What matters most is how you *bounce back.*

🚦 Step 1: Pause (Without Judgment)

The first step is simply to **pause**.

Not to panic, not to beat yourself up, but to acknowledge the moment with kindness.

Take a breath.

🧘 *"I made a choice. I can learn from it. I'm still moving forward."*

Now, take another breath.

Your budgeting journey isn't about never making mistakes; it's about building *resilience* and *awareness.*

We're human, and humans make mistakes. You can own this and push through it.

🔍 Step 2: Reflect — What Was Really Happening?

Now let's get curious (not critical). Use this moment as a data point.

Ask yourself:

- **What was I feeling before I spent?**
  Stressed, tired, lonely, bored?

- **What did I actually need?**
  Comfort, escape, connection, rest?

- **What could I try next time instead?**
  Call a friend, journal, go for a walk, make a cup of tea?

> 💬 **Example**
>
> *"I spent $70 online after a rough day at work. I think I really needed to vent and decompress, not another pair of jeans."*

These answers give you power. They help you build emotional awareness, not emotional shame.

🍿 Step 3: Take a Micro-Action

A "whoops" doesn't mean you're off track, but taking one small *corrective* step can help you re-ground and feel more in control again quickly.

Pick just one:

- Move $5 into savings

- Update your tracker or spending log

- Revisit your goals or your "why" statement

- Prep dinner instead of ordering in

- Re-read your budget or money reset plan

Even the *tiniest* course correction helps rewire your brain from "I blew it" to "I'm learning."

✅ Action Step

Consider creating an **Emotional Spending Journal** to record your moments. It could be as simple as a single piece of paper, or a leather-bound volume with gilded pages (I know which I'd prefer, but I'm a book nerd).

Include in your journalling:

- The purchase

- What triggered it

- How you felt before and after

- One thing you'll try next time

- The micro-action you took to help you feel more in control

💛 Give Yourself a Break

First, Choose Compassion. Always.

You are *not* your bank balance.

You are *not* your spending slip-ups.

You are *not* a bad person.

You are a human being learning new habits, and that's messy, emotional, and entirely normal.

Let go of the guilt spiral.

Shame makes you want to avoid your finances. Compassion helps you *face them*. And that's what creates change.

Instead of saying:

> ✗ *"I'm terrible with money."*

> Try:

> ✓ *"That was a tough moment. I'm learning what triggered it. I don't need to be perfect. I need to be honest, kind to myself, and willing to keep showing up."*

This is about *progress*, not perfection. The goal isn't to never emotionally spend again, it's to understand yourself better each time you do.

🛡️ Build Gentle Guardrails

Compassion is half the equation. The other half? Putting systems in place that make it *easier* to do what you want and *harder* to derail yourself.

Here are a few **gentle, beginner-friendly guardrails** you can try:

🕐 1. The 24-Hour Rule

Before buying anything non-essential, give yourself a full day to sit on the decision. You might still buy it, but you'll do so with intention.

📋 2. Create a "30-Day List"

Instead of impulse buying, add the item to a note or list titled *"Things I'm Thinking About."* Revisit it in 30 days. Most of the time, the urge has passed.

💳 3. Unlink Your Cards

Remove saved cards from shopping apps or browsers. The extra friction between seeing and purchasing gives your rational brain time to catch up with your emotional one.

📱 4. Use App Limits or Website Blockers

Set screen time limits on shopping apps or block access during known emotional spending windows (like late at night or weekends).

🛝 5. Give Yourself "Play Money"

Set a small "play money" amount each week, fortnight, or month. It's guilt-free, budgeted, and helps curb unplanned splurges. Besides, this is your money. You're an adult who can do adult things. *You are allowed to have some fun!*

✨ Reminder

Guardrails are not punishments. They're *supports* you choose to make your future self's life easier.

Every time you use one, you're strengthening your self-trust.

🌟

You've Got This!

This isn't about never spending emotionally again. It's about learning, growing, and building better habits with kindness.

You're not broken. Emotional spending is just a signal, not a flaw.

The more awareness and compassion you bring to it, the more control you take back.

🎁 Bonus 3: Money Confidence Scripts

Know what to say when money talks get tough.

📘 Why This Matters

Money conversations can be uncomfortable, but they're also where *real empowerment* happens.

Whether it's negotiating a bill, setting boundaries with a partner, or asking for support during a tough time, **you deserve to feel confident speaking up.** These simple, respectful scripts help you break the ice, stay calm, and communicate clearly, even when your heart's racing.

You don't need to be perfect. You just need a starting point. These are yours.

✨ What You'll Get

- Scripts to negotiate with providers
- Templates for conversations with housemates, partners, or family
- A checklist for debt collection calls or hardship requests

🔋 Script Section 1: Negotiating with Providers

Negotiating with service providers can feel intimidating, especially if you've never done it before. But here's a secret: **they expect you to ask**.

Phone, internet, streaming, energy, insurance; these companies are in *competitive* markets. They often have secret offers, loyalty deals, or hardship support that they won't volunteer unless you ask.

This isn't about being pushy; it's about *self-advocacy*. You're simply saying, "I want to stay with you, but I need a better deal."

And it works.

🎯 When to Use These Scripts

- When your contract has expired
- If you've been with a provider for 6+ months
- When a competitor offers a cheaper rate
- During tough financial periods (requesting hardship support)

🔍 Before You Call

Have these ready:

- Your latest bill or plan details
- A calm, respectful tone
- *Optional:* a competitor's offer you've seen online

You don't need to threaten to leave. Just express your situation honestly.

📝 Sample Scripts

- "Hi, I'm reviewing my bills and would like to check if there are any discounts, offers, or loyalty options available right now."

- "I've been a customer for a while and I'd really like to stay, but I need to reduce my costs. Are there any better plans available?"

- "I've seen some other offers and want to check if you're able to match or beat them before I make a decision."

🛠️ Script Modifiers (Use What Feels Right!)

- "I'm going through a tight patch — do you have any temporary support options?"

- "I don't need all the extras. Can you simplify this plan to lower the cost?"

- "Before I cancel, I just want to check if there's a better offer you can apply."

✅ Action Step

Make one negotiation call this week. It could save you $10 - $50 per month in less than 10 minutes.

Journal Prompt (optional):

What did I notice about how I felt before and after the call?

_____

_____

_____

_____

🏡 Script Section 2: Talking to Housemates, Partners, or Family

Money can be one of the most emotionally loaded topics in our closest relationships. But silence, resentment, or avoidance usually makes it worse.

Clear, kind communication builds **trust, fairness, and teamwork** whether you're splitting rent, managing bills, or sharing financial goals. And good news: you don't have to be a financial expert to start these conversations. You just need a little confidence and a script that feels natural.

This section helps you open the door without drama.

🎯 When to Use This Script

- You want to split shared expenses more fairly

- You've taken on more than your share and need to reset

- You want to start budgeting *together*, not in isolation

- You're ready to align on goals or habits as a team

📃 Sample Scripts

Pick a tone that suits your relationship whether warm, direct, or casual. You're not accusing; you're inviting collaboration.

- "Hey, I've been thinking about how we handle bills. Can we have a quick chat about making it feel more balanced?"

- "I'm working on my budget and would love for us to have a system that works for both of us; something that's clear and easy."

- "Would you be open to a money check-in once a month? Just something casual to stay on the same page."

⋯ Optional Follow-Ups

- "What feels fair to you?"

- "Is there anything you've been worried about or wanted to change too?"

- "Can we brainstorm a system that works for both of us?"

⚖️ Sample Situations

Situation	Possible Script
You've been covering most shared costs	"I've been covering a few things lately and it's starting to stretch me. Can we look at how we're splitting things?"
You're moving in together	"Before we move in, I'd love to talk about how we'll handle expenses so we're both clear from the start."
Your partner overspends	"I noticed we're going over budget a bit. Can we talk about how we want to approach spending together?"
You want to team up on a goal	"I'm trying to build an emergency fund. Want to make it a challenge we do together?"

✅ Action Step

Pick one conversation you've been avoiding and write your version of a script for it below:

📘 *My conversation starter:*

_____

_____

_____

_____

_____

Then practice it out loud or roleplay it with a trusted friend.

✨ Reminder

You're not being dramatic. You're being responsible.

And if it feels awkward, that's okay. That's just the sound of **new boundaries being born.**

📞 Script Section 3: Debt Collection & Hardship Calls

Getting a call (or letter) from a debt collector can feel overwhelming and scary. But you still have rights, choices, and **the power to lead the conversation**.

You don't need to panic, overshare, or agree to something on the spot. With the right script and a few key phrases, you can pause the pressure, protect your peace, and negotiate with confidence.

In addition to this, if you have received a call (or letter) from a debt collector, a great place to start would be to contact a Financial Counsellor. They are the experts and can help you 100% free of charge.

You can find a Financial Counsellor by doing a simple Google search for Financial Counsellors in your local area, call the National Debt Helpline on 1800 007 007 or use their website (www.ndh.org.au) to find local services.

But if you feel confident that you can tackle this yourself, this section gives you a calm, clear starting point.

🎯 When to Use These Scripts

- A debt collector contacts you about a debt

- You're struggling with a loan, credit card, or bill

- You want to request a payment plan or pause

- You're unsure what your options are but need to buy time

⚠️ Important Phrases to Remember

- "I'm not in a position to make a payment today."

- "Please provide all details in writing."

- "I'd like to apply for hardship support."

- "Can we set up a realistic plan that won't cause further hardship?"

💡 Tip

You don't have to and shouldn't agree to anything on the spot. Ask for everything in writing and tell them you'll get back to them.

📞 Sample Script for Debt Collection Contact

- "Hi, I just received a message about this debt and I'm reviewing the details. Can you please send me the full breakdown in writing, including the amount owed, the original creditor, and any fees added?"

- "At this stage, I'm not making a payment or agreement over the phone, but I would like to review the documents and be in touch."

🤝 Script for Requesting Hardship Support

- "Hi, I'm currently experiencing financial hardship and would like to discuss what support options are available, such as a pause or payment plan."

- "I want to stay on track with my obligations, but I need a plan that reflects my current situation."

- "Can you please outline your hardship policy and what documents I may need to provide?"

✏️ Keep a Record

Use the Debt Demolition section of your workbook or a separate page to log:

- Who you spoke to

- The date and time

- What was discussed

- Any reference numbers or outcomes

✅ Action Step

If you're currently behind on a bill or debt, take these steps:

- First, **contact a Financial Counsellor** in your local area and make an appointment

- Call the provider and use a hardship script

- Respond to a collector with a request for written info

You're not a "bad person" for needing help.

Life happens. The key is to face it calmly and take small, empowered steps.

You can find a Financial Counsellor by doing a simple Google search for Financial Counsellors in your local area, call the National Debt Helpline on 1800 007 007 or use their website (www.ndh.org.au) to find local services.

📋 Debt Call Checklist

Prepare. Call. Record. Follow Up.

Use this checklist before, during, and after your call to stay calm and in control.

📥 Before the Call

- ☐ Locate any paperwork or emails about the debt
- ☐ Write down your key facts (amount owed, due date, etc.)
- ☐ Prepare a short script (e.g., "I'm requesting hardship support")
- ☐ Have a notepad or digital doc ready to take notes
- ☐ Take a deep breath; this is just a step, not a crisis

📞 During the Call

- ☐ Ask for the caller's name, company, and contact details
- ☐ Confirm the details of the debt (amount, original creditor, due date)
- ☐ Stay calm — you don't have to explain your whole life
- ☐ Use clear language:
  - ○ "I'm not able to make a payment today."
  - ○ "Please send everything to me in writing."
  - ○ "I'd like to request a hardship arrangement."
- ☐ Avoid agreeing to anything you can't afford or haven't reviewed
- ☐ Take notes, especially if they offer a plan or request documents

📪 After the Call

- ☐ Write down the date, time, and who you spoke with
- ☐ Save any documents or emails they send
- ☐ If needed, send a follow-up request in writing (email is fine)
- ☐ Schedule a check-in for your next payment or review date
- ☐ Give yourself credit: you took action today and that's not easy

🌟

You've Got This!

This bonus wasn't just about scripts; it was about building your **financial voice**.

Every time you speak up, ask a question, or state your needs, you grow your confidence.

And *that* is money power.

You made it!

Whether you did this over 30 days or all in one week, you now have a foundation for long-term financial wellness.

You reset your mindset, built a budget, faced your debt, grew savings, and started building wealth.

You've done the hard part, now keep the momentum going.

You've got this!